LEAN UX AND SCRUM - LEADING APPROACHES TO AGILE DESIGN AND AGILE DEVELOPMENT SUCCESSFULLY COMBINED

A PREPARATION FOR THE "PROFESSIONAL SCRUM™ WITH USER EXPERIENCE (PSU I)" CERTIFICATION EXAM

PAUL C. MüLLER

Made with ♥ on the Notion Press Platform
www.notionpress.com

Contents

Foreword

Generalization is not a new phenomenon. Often, when we think of concepts, we actually mean specific examples that belong to those concepts. For example, when we think of "tool" most people first think of "hammer", when we think of "color" we think of "red", or when we think of "instrument" we think of "violin".

We know it quite similarly in the agile context. When talking about an agile method, many people think of Scrum, although Scrum is not characterized as a method, but as a framework and several hundred other agile approaches, methods and frameworks are known. In the same way, a large number of people in Germany think of Design Thinking when they hear the keyword "agile innovation method" - in some other countries, there are partly other methods, frameworks and approaches, which already proves that Design Thinking is not remotely the only agile innovation method.

Since February 2019, Scrum.org, one of the world's leading certification institutes for Scrum professionals, has been offering a certification with the short name PSU (Professional Scrum with User Experience), which has already been obtained by more than 1500 people by fall 2021. The focus is on a specific agile innovation approach in combination with Scrum: "Lean UX". This approach can be coordinated with the Scrum approach in an impressive way. Here, the innovation process is not carried out first, the results of which are then to be implemented within the framework of Scrum, but the innovation process runs quasi parallel to the Scrum process. There is mutual support and mutual learning from both directions. A major advantage of this is that innovation and implementation are thus actual agile partners and we do not fall into the "waterfall trap", where (for example, through design thinking) a kind of specification is developed, which is then implemented through Scrum.

This book has two goals: On the one hand, it is intended to provide an introduction to the combination of Lean UX with Scrum, and on the other hand, it includes the information necessary for a successful Scrum PSU certification exam according to our experience and can thus also be used for exam preparation.

Since this book is NOT a publication of Scrum.org and no persons of the organization were involved in its creation, no responsibility can be taken for whether the certification organization may develop further questions in the course of time, which are not presented in this book. The information gathered is to the best of my knowledge and experience over many years with the approaches described.

The author

Preface

Acknowledgements

This book was written based on various sources and years of experience in using Scrum and various other agile methodologies and frameworks, including Lean UX and Design Thinking. Its content reflects the author's experience only and has not been authorized or released by the rights holders or developers of said methodologies. Thus, the content has no official character. Nevertheless, the content of this book has been compiled in such a way that it is suitable as a source for preparing for the Professional Scrum™ with User Experience (PSU I) certification exam. The corresponding trademark is owned by Scrum.org. Further use of trademark identification and the like has been omitted from the text. However, they are always considered to be included.

The author cannot assume any guarantees for the further developments of the certifier regarding exam contents (questions, rules). The contents of this book were created at the time of writing based on the information available and prepared to the best of our knowledge for the readership and potential examinees of the said certification exam.

This text deliberately does not delve into the basics of understanding Scrum. Rather, it is assumed that people seeking PSU-I certification have sufficient knowledge of Scrum, such as is presented in the context of PSM, PSPO or PSD certifications. If you do not have such knowledge, acquiring this basic knowledge is recommended for the full benefit of the book content.

ONE

INTRODUCTION TO LEAN UX

Lean User Experience, or Lean UX for short, is an approach that encompasses mindset, culture and processes from the Lean and Agile contexts and aims to design solutions of maximum customer value. It proceeds in small steps and the hypotheses developed therein are verified immediately. In doing so, Lean UX design expands the traditional role of UX, which has often been limited to performing design and anticipating user interaction, to include important topics such as asking whether a feature makes sense and is necessary, determining what functions are required in the process, and estimating the benefits that can be achieved with it. The goal is to better understand whether a system meets its intended business goals through immediate feedback.

Lean UX, unlike a large number of innovation methods, works with an approach that does not strive to create the concept before development begins - as was necessary in the context of earlier software development, since a final product was eventually delivered as part of fixed releases, for example on CDs. In the context of modern software development approaches, which support approaches such as continuous development, integration and delivery, it is more purposeful for the UX and development processes to run in parallel. This involves combining techniques and methods from different sources and frameworks. The most important of these include user experience design, lean thinking concepts, design thinking, agile software development approaches, and lean startup.

The principles of Lean UX

Lean UX defines a set of principles for team organization, corporate culture and approach. These form the basic framework of the approach on which processes, methods and responsibilities are based.

Principles for the organization of the teams

The principles for organizing teams define the requirements that are necessary on the team side in order to achieve maximum success with Lean UX. Both requirements for the team itself and the necessary framework conditions that the team must find are addressed. The principles are called:

- Interdisciplinary teams
- Compact, purpose-built and location-based teams
- Independent and authorized teams
- Problem focused teams

Interdisciplinary teams

By interdisciplinary teams, we first understand teams that are composed of experts with the most diverse backgrounds, so that real synergy can be created through the coming together of the most diverse experiences and knowledge. It is not only thought in terms of individual methods, departments, etc., but by working together and combining the most diverse approaches and experiences, new, more far-reaching approaches to solutions can be developed.

In fact, this is only the first step. An interdisciplinary team that wants to make the best possible use of synergies also needs the various participants to get to grips with each other's topics and areas of expertise to such an extent that they understand each other's approaches and considerations and can discuss and evaluate them with each other. This is the only way to achieve real synergy. However, this process generally takes time and is part of the team's development.

Compact, purpose-built and location-based teams

Communication and collaboration are key success factors. In teams that are too large, collaboration and communication become difficult. Team sizes of around 5-6 people are ideal; this provides a good basis for diversity without making communication difficult because of too large a team size. In any case, teams should also be physically in the same location, as collaboration is optimal when it happens together. Technically supported processes of physically distributed teams always lead to a loss in communication and collaboration and thus usually also in terms of the jointly developed solution approaches and topics. Teams should be put together in relation to concrete issues. Standard teams that address and deal with a wide variety of issues are often less useful in practice.

Independent and authorized teams

UX teams should be able to work independently, self-organized and equipped with the necessary authority. They need infrastructure and tools to work well and must be able to interact with users and customers to generate new input and feedback on which to execute and develop their work.

Problem focused teams

The focus of a successful UX team should always be on the results to be achieved and the associated benefits (outcome) and not on the short-term addition to existing products (output). Otherwise, there is too great a risk of not really innovating, but either just mimicking the competition or slightly improving existing functionality, which generally does not lead to significant benefits. Instead, a UX team should think through topics and problem areas from a customer and user perspective in a completely new way and, based on this, find innovative solutions that solve problems in a novel way and thus offer real added value to the intended user group.

Principles of corporate culture

Regardless of which agile approach or which agile framework is involved, many organizations still live under the misconception that agility can be pushed onto a few people, that an agile team can be deployed for innovation or product development (for example, with Scrum), and that the entire organization can continue to operate as before. In fact, this is possible, but it destroys a significant portion of the benefits and impact of agile teams and reduces the use of agility to the introduction of a few new methods.

Only when agility actually influences the corporate culture and the way of working together in the team, but also across hierarchies, is actually lived, will the benefits of agile methods and frameworks also be realizable. The associated principles are called:

- From doubt to security
- Progress = results instead of throughput
- Minimize waste
- Create common understanding
- No rock stars, gurus and ninjas
- Allow failures

From doubt to security

Innovative processes are usually based on assumptions whose correctness must first be tested and evaluated. As a result, some assumptions also turn out to be wrong. Real progress is only possible through a continuous process based on experiments and their evaluation and the associated feedback. This also requires an appropriate mindset and an understanding of errors and assumptions that turn out to be incorrect.

Progress = results instead of throughput

The goal of an innovation process is not to develop a multitude of improvements and additional functions to existing solutions, but to achieve an additional benefit for the customer, which in turn leads to either the customer buying again or new customers being acquired. This approach can, of course, also lead to the implementation of new functions. The important thing here is that the focus is not on inflating a feature list, but on providing actual benefits. Thus, the benefit or progress of an innovation process is measured by the additional benefit achieved for the customer, but not by which (or how many) additional functions have been developed.

Minimize waste

"More is more" - this somewhat platitudinous statement seems to be the maxim in many development departments, especially in the technical environment. As a result, requirements specifications are becoming longer and longer, with the existing being dragged on within the framework of grandfathering, even if the benefit achieved by this is not given or is only marginal.

A concept that originated in the context of lean is called "just well enough". This means that solutions are not particularly beneficial if they contain all conceivable features, but rather if they offer optimal benefits for reasonable costs. This leads to the omission of possible features that do not contribute sufficiently to value creation for the customer.

Create common understanding

A major challenge in agile teams is always the requirement that the participants have a common idea of what is important and valuable for the customer or user. Far too often we fall into the trap of seeing requirements only from our point of view - based on our own ideas, experiences and needs.

Alignment in the team, i.e. the creation of a common understanding of the project assignment and the goal to be achieved, is essential. This is especially important in a team that is largely self-directed in its approach. Without a common vision, there is a great risk that the process will disintegrate into a multitude of individual initiatives that address and seek to answer very different questions. The creation of synergy and the associated gain in knowledge tend to fall by the wayside.

No rock stars, gurus and ninjas

Agile approaches are based on the strength and cooperation of teams that bring in different skills and knowledge. They are thus the counter-model to the lone genius who hatches ingenious ideas and products in a quiet chamber. In fact, when putting together teams, we do not so much strive to include the best specialists possible, but rather to bring together people with very different experiences and knowledge, who work together as a team to find solutions to problems.

An important success factor here is the creation of synergies. This is based on the conviction that even the best specialist will only contribute the (albeit quite distinctive) experience and knowledge of a single person, whereas several people, even those who are not quite as experienced, will contribute a multitude of experiences and opinions and thus in sum - by working together synergistically - can make better contributions to solutions than a single person. The prerequisite for this is the willingness to work together as a team.

Allow failures

Organizations in which making mistakes is viewed exclusively negatively - and where the focus in such cases is more on finding someone to blame than on fixing the mistake - will not be able to successfully apply agile methods. Even worse, in many companies, committing mistakes means that employees expose themselves and may face dismissal or other losses in terms of their job as a result. In such an environment, a lot of time is spent hiding errors, which often results in errors being discovered only when they require significant effort to fix, whereas immediate action might have caused a fraction of the damage and cost.

In fact, a central success factor of all agile methods is conducting experiments. We recognize a situation that is not optimal and for which improvement seems to make sense, and together we decide to try out a solution approach. Since this is a new approach, there is of course the possibility that it will not bring the expected success or possibly cannot even be carried out in the intended way. Nevertheless, it is important. Even in the case of failure, it provides us with an important insight and thus moves us further along the path to improvement. But where people are afraid of making mistakes because they are threatened with the corresponding sanctions, we risk that no further development will be pursued or that this will only take place in such small steps that we will inevitably fall behind the development of the market more and more.

Principles of the approach

The principles related to the approach describe the ideal framework and procedures for carrying out the UX process. They include:

- Using small batch sizes to reduce risk
- Continuous Learning (Continuous Discovery)
- GOOB (Getting Out Of the Building) as an approach to ensure user-centricity.
- Externalize work
- Realize instead of analyze
- Away from the deliverables

Using small batch sizes to reduce risk

Many teams work on task blocks or work packages that are far too large. This increases the risk in several ways. On the one hand, larger tasks very often also mean greater complexity, which in itself entails a greater risk of errors. In addition, it has been shown that a large work package that is described is described in much less detail than if this large work package were subdivided.

Specifically, if we have a large work package or task that we describe by additional information, or else we divide the large package into, say, 5 subpackages, we find in most cases that the number of attributes and additional information of the 5 subpackages together is often several times the number of attributes or additional information of the requirement that is not subdivided.

This is due to the fact that smaller packages are easier to imagine and accordingly the "right questions" can be asked and answered sooner, whereas large tasks often have a high level of complexity, which means that we are not even aware of all the relevant sub-questions. This leads to the fact that the people in the implementation also have less information, which potentially leads to more errors and more queries during the implementation process.

We thus prefer clear task sizes. They not only offer less risk, but also more motivation because they can also be completed better and in a more goal-oriented manner. Finally, tasks completed in this way can in turn lead to feedback and knowledge gain sooner, which additionally optimizes the project and the associated activities.

Continuous Learning (Continuous Discovery)

Continuous learning does not mean learning any content in the quiet study room, but represents an essential approach in the further development of the team on the one hand and the solution approach on the other. It is about involving the stakeholders involved, such as customers, users, etc., in the design and development process and learning from each other.

Agile development and agile design are based on the notion of continuous cooperation between the business side (customers, users, external experts, etc.) and the implementation side (design and/or development team). Both contribute some of the necessary knowledge and experience. But only the combination of both leads to optimal results: those that combine the benefit for the stakeholders with the technical excellence brought in by the implementation side.

GOOB (Getting Out Of the Building) as an approach to ensure user-centricity.

The acronym "GOOB" goes back to Stanford professor, author and entrepreneur Steve Blank. His demand was that the team should not hatch theories and ideas about the user and his needs in some conference room, but that these should be gained directly from and with the actual expert, the user. For this, continuous collaboration with a lot of transparency and feedback is essential as a basis for further steps. In essence, it is about leaving the quiet study room and learning in contact with users - whether in direct conversation or through the use of analytical methods - based on reality and developing theories that can subsequently be verified.

Externalize work

The principle of externalizing work must also be seen in the same context. It is about making work results transparent, showing them and obtaining feedback for them. It is about being inspired by each other and building on the ideas of others. It is not important who had the idea originally, but that we gain additional, new insights through the different knowledge and experiences in the team, but also beyond that, and thus find new, better ideas and approaches to solutions.

Realize instead of analyze

Instead of extensively exchanging ideas and theories and pitting opinion against opinion, we implement ideas and theories in the form of prototypes, mockups, etc., and use these products to verify our theories by conducting experiments and gathering feedback from real (potential) users. This gives us a reliable source of insight and allows us to build on solid ground.

Away from the deliverables

As indicated earlier, the measure of the success of a UX initiative is the benefit it realizes or enables for the customer. It is not the number of innovations and additional functions that is relevant here, but their significance for the customer.

TWO
THE LEAN UX PROCESS

The Lean UX process is initially divided into two basic parts, which are also known from approaches such as design thinking. First, the problem and the issue must be understood, and then insights and finally solutions are developed by means of creative methods and their verification. The individual sub-processes can be described as follows:

- Hypothesizing
- Collaborative design
- MVP and experiments
- Feedback and research

A central aspect when we work with Lean UX (but also with various other agile innovation approaches) is to focus not on concrete deliverables (output) but on achieving results (outcomes). Thus, the point of using Lean UX is not to add as much additional functionality as possible to an existing product, but to achieve benefits and outcomes for the customer. This can possibly lead to additional functionality; however, there is also the possibility of discovering completely new approaches through the use of innovative approaches, which lead to serving the requirements and needs in a completely different way better than ever before and thus also realizing an innovative advantage in the market.

Hypothesizing

The first step in the "hypothesis generation" sub-process is to formulate assumptions on which further work is to be based. To this end, the first step is to obtain and review the materials needed for further research - such as analyses, reports, previous approaches to solutions, and stakeholder analyses.

Based on this, assumptions are now formulated with regard to the actual situation and the target situation. A worksheet often used in this context goes back to Giff Constable. It distinguishes business assumptions from assumptions about the user(s) and is presented in the book by Jeff Gothelf and Josh Seiden:

Business Assumptions:

1. I think my customers need ...
2. These requirements can be met with ....
3. My first customers are (or will be) ...
4. The biggest value my customers want to get out of my service is ...
5. The customer can also benefit from these additional advantages ...
6. I will acquire the majority of my customers through ....
7. I will earn money through ...
8. My main competition in the market will be ....
9. We will knock them out of the field for the following reasons ...
10. My biggest product risk is ...
11. We will solve this by ...
12. We will know we have succeeded when customer behavior changes as follows: ...
13. What other assumptions do we have that, if proven wrong, would cause our business / product to fail? ...

User Assumptions:

1. Who is the user?
2. How does our product fit into his work / life?
3. What problems does our product solve?
4. When and how is our product used?
5. Which features are important?
6. How should our product look and behave?

Of course, this is only an example and other questions can be created and used depending on the question and objective. The only important thing is that this provides a list of assumptions from which relevant hypotheses can be derived in a next step. These form the basis for further considerations. Of course, it can also turn out that assumptions were wrong, which also leads us to a gain in knowledge. Again and again, we find that products and services are built with regard to assumed requirements and wishes of the customer, which ultimately turn out not to exist - or not to a sufficient degree. Accordingly, it is important to identify these false assumptions at an early stage and to draw the right conclusions from them.

Assumptions are initially simply opinions, which are based on more or less experience and knowledge. They often say more about the world view and perception of the person who formulates them than about the reality described in them. Accordingly, in a next step we have to transform the assumptions into a format that is verifiable. This format is called "hypothesis". A general format for formulating a hypothesis might be:

We believe that <assertion> is true. We will know if we are <right/wrong> when we receive the following feedback:

<quantitative feedback> and/or

<qualitative feedback> and/or

<change in the relevant indicator>

Many methods and techniques can be used to evaluate the hypotheses, which are applied in a wide variety of approaches.

Since a large number of assumptions usually also results in a large number of hypotheses and their verification is often associated with corresponding effort, it has proven useful to prioritize the verification of the hypotheses. In this context, different aspects can be of importance for prioritization (as we are also familiar with, for example, in the context of prioritization of product backlog items by a product owner in Scrum): Value creation for the customer, risk associated with the hypothesis if the hypothesis is not true, possibly a system-immanent dependency of individual hypotheses on each other, etc.

Persona building

In the context of hypothesis generation, the formation of personas is often approached - if not already available elsewhere in the company. Personas represent (future) users of our product or service. These are not real people, but rather people that we develop - based on our questions - in relation to real customer groups and that can also evolve continuously in the course of the work due to our constant growth in knowledge. We use personas in the course of the innovation process (and often in other contexts as well) in order to gain an empathetic approach to understanding our (future) customers in addition to facts and figures, and thus also to better identify any existing obstacles and motivators.

In the context of Lean UX, we often speak of proto-personas to show that we use a simpler, more pragmatic approach in their creation than is often the case with personas created partly externally by service providers. In particular, the resulting proto-personas are also more clearly aligned with our questions and not generic to a wide variety of contexts, which in turn enables a focus.

Proto-personas always have a real name (not Max Mustermann). Care should be taken to ensure that these are not names of people we know (customers, celebrities, etc.), otherwise the risk of mutual influence and blurring becomes too great. In addition, they include behavioral demographic information, information about their problems and needs, specifically sharpened with regard to our topics, as well as potential solutions and other information that helps us to develop the most beneficial solutions for this particular persona(s).

The development process often proceeds in four stages:

1. Brainstorming in the team
2. Narrowing down the collected ideas to 3-4 personas based on the set requirements
3. Completion of the personas in the team
4. Involve external colleagues to further complement the personas and make them more realistic.

In the context of working with personas, we should always ask ourselves whether the persona is really realistic and purposeful and whether our creativity has not run away with us. We should then ask ourselves whether the requirements and obstacles underlying the initiative are at all relevant for the persona developed and whether it would be willing to become active for a corresponding solution (for example, to buy our product).

Collaborative design

Jeff Gothelf defines user experience as the totality of all interactions that a user performs with a product or service. Very different aspects come into play here, on the one hand because of the diversity of the requirements placed on the product itself, and on the other hand because of the diversity of the users and their use cases. This makes it particularly important that the problem is viewed and worked on from a wide variety of viewpoints. In short: synergetic teamwork is of crucial importance.

From the perspective of Lean UX, but also fundamentally from the perspective of agile and/or lean-based approaches, there is a certain attitude of entitlement towards the team. It is of great importance that this is a team that actually works together and understands that the best results are achieved when everyone contributes their knowledge and skills and solutions are developed from the synergy of this.

What has no place in such a context are hero-based approaches in which one person virtually leads the way and makes the rest of the team the vicarious agent. Even the best and most experienced professional will never contribute the same diversity and level of experience and knowledge as the entirety of the team. More diverse, sustainable, and often innovative approaches emerge. In addition, "heroes" are often characterized by rapid change. They move from one project to the next (or are assigned to one project after another), representing one-off solutions rather than continuous, experience-based, customer-centric development.

A typical approach to team collaboration is that ideas are first contributed by team members, which are discussed and evaluated together. It is decided which ones will be pursued further. Other team members contribute additions or extensions, which are also evaluated in turn. In this way, the topic continues to develop, always based on the insights of the others and a shared way of thinking and being creative.

Once solutions have been found, they are then fleshed out with low-fidelity sketches or wireframes. However, this is still done very simply and is intended to allow everyone to contribute and changes to the process are easily possible. In this way, approaches can also be reviewed and supplemented, or discarded and reapproached. One of the biggest risks in this phase is that people fall in love with "their solution" and want to see it implemented - for whatever reason - instead of being willing to learn from others and perceive their own ideas as part of a whole, better solution.

One method that is often used in this context is the Charette method. However, there are of course many others that can produce equally good results.

The Charette process

For a goal-oriented implementation of a Charette procedure, sufficient time should be available - at least half a working day, depending on the task also significantly more - as well as an undisturbed room with sufficient space, tables and a wall on which the team's progress can be visualized transparently for all participants. As materials, there should be sufficient pens and colors of various kinds as well as large blank DIN A3 or DIN A2 sheets and materials such as are usually found in moderation sets.

Charette teams with 5-8 people are ideal. In the case of larger teams, it makes sense to divide them into sub-teams. At the end of the session, the results of the sub-teams are compared with each other and, if necessary, findings are combined. When working with personas, these should be well known to all participants in advance.

The procedure itself can be divided into 5 phases:

- Problem definition
- Individual idea generation
- Presentation and meeting
- Iteration and optimization
- Idea generation in the team

Problem definition

A fundamental prerequisite for the success of any activity and any method is that all participants know the problem as well as any known existing constraints. We dedicate ourselves to this task in the problem definition phase. Between 15-45 minutes are available for this (depending on complexity, team size, etc.) and methods used here include presentations, discussions, etc., as well as techniques geared to this task.

Individual idea generation

A very common measure for individual idea generation is the 6-panel design grid. For this, about 10 minutes are available and the individual team members work individually with a sheet of paper divided into 6 fields (2x3) (usually DIN-A3 or larger). Alternatively, work can also be done on individual, small whiteboards.

In each of the six fields, the persona (if none is used, customer groups, customers, etc. are also possible) and the problem or issue to be addressed for said persona are entered in the margin. Personas and problems can be used several times in different combinations. Based on this, "low-fidelity sketches" with a solution approach are to be created in the fields. A total of about 5 minutes are available for this. It is about spontaneous sketching and not about long thinking and consideration and also not about creative perfection. A few strokes are usually enough for a sketch. Even if someone "can't draw", they should still draw here and do without text or the like, since drawing - even if the result is difficult to recognize - addresses other areas of the brain that support the creativity of this step better than if approaches are verbalized.

Presentation and meeting

Each team member presents their work in 3 minutes (per person, not per solution approach). For each topic, a brief description is given of who and for which problem the solution approach is intended, followed by a short description of the solution.

Based on this, the team gives feedback, which is not an evaluation, but asking questions that help to better understand the approach.

Iteration and optimization

Now the task is to jointly revise the various approaches. To do this, the participants form pairs that further revise the design proposals at hand. If two people had similar ideas, it makes sense for them to form a pair together.

Approximately 10 minutes are available for a first phase in which the pairs decide what they want to change and what they want to keep. The goal here is to pick up the most promising idea and elaborate on it. The original six ideas should be presented on a single A3 sheet based on the feedback received. Another 10 minutes are available for this second part. The time boxes are helpful because they should help to ensure that the work is focused and that the participants do not get lost in detailed work.

Idea generation in the team

While individual brainstorming was about generating a multitude of ideas, approaches and points of view, team brainstorming is now again about focusing on a single idea that is to be pursued further. This is referred to as the convergence phase. Approximately 45 minutes are available for this. The team agrees on a single, final idea which it finds most promising and which is worthy of serving as the basis for the next steps of the UX process.

The various ideas and the associated workflow are visualized and, for example, sketched on a flipchart pad and pinned to the whiteboard. A common consensus is formed, whereby it is also possible to make cuts and prioritize. Ideas that are not currently being pursued further, but are too good to simply throw away, are placed in an idea parking area so that they can be picked up again later if necessary. A decision is made in the meeting as to which approach will be pursued. If several teams have been working in parallel, the various sub-teams present their choices and from this a final choice is determined for the overall team. The decision reached is documented on the wall so that it can be referred to at any time.

The use of (existing) design systems

The uxdesign.cc website defines a design system as follows:

"A Design System is the single source of truth which groups all the elements that will allow the teams to design, realize and develop a product. [1]"

When we look at larger organizations in particular, we often find existing design systems that have either grown over time or have been created by external service providers and implement a standard, so to speak. This can be very supportive, but also always carries a risk - depending on quality and design framework - of limiting creativity.

One could say that design systems are, so to speak, evolved style guides, although they can often also be found under terms such as "style guide", "pattern library", "brand guidelines", "asset library" or similar. One example that is publicly available is the U.S. government's design system: https://designsystem.digital.gov/

We use design systems to focus results after the relatively abstract work in the innovation process and break them down to the level of detail, so to speak.

Advantages of design systems include:

- By using a design system, faster progress is possible because existing elements are used and not everything has to be developed from scratch.
- A prototype build can be done more efficiently based on building blocks.
- A uniform appearance in the team is supported.
- Centralized design enables higher quality at lower cost.

A disadvantage is that what is not provided for by the design system can be made impossible or hindered, if necessary, and thus certain innovations can be slowed down - with which there is a certain risk of putting the brakes on creativity.

Typically included in style guides / design systems:

- Logos
- Page elements: Header, Footer, Grid Structures
- Typographic specifications
- Form layout
- Field sizes and positioning of fields
- Labels
- Menu structures and contents
- Color palette/s
- Text style
- a. o.

MVP and experiments

The third phase of the Lean UX process is about implementing the approaches developed in the Collaborative Design phase in a way that allows to achieve qualitatively valuable feedback. Prototypes at different levels of detail can be used for this purpose. Alternatively or in parallel, an approach originally known from the books of Eric Ries and his Lean Startup concept is also implemented.

MVP approach and Lean Startup

The emergence of the MVP approach is usually located in the context of the startup scene. Too often, it is observed that innovative people or small businesses fall in love with their product in such a way that they (almost) ruin themselves to develop it and bring it to market. They trust that - if they value their product so much - the whole world must feel the same way and the product will recoup all investments with ease.

Unfortunately, this is not the case in practice. Even large corporations with huge marketing and analysis departments repeatedly bring out products that do not appeal to any market or only to a very small one and become a loss-making business for the producer. If it is a small organization or even a private person, such a misjudgement can lead to the producer ruining himself completely and in many cases having to pay for his misjudgement for years to come.

In the context, Eric Ries formulated:

"Lean Startup promotes the timely production of prototypes to verify assumed market assumptions, as well as the utilization of customer feedback on these prototypes for the purpose of significantly faster further development than is possible with traditional software engineering methods [...]. By contacting real users more frequently and weeding out incorrect market assumptions as early as possible, lean startup processes reduce wasted resources."

The technique used for this is called the MVP approach (where MVP stands for Minimum Viable Product, i.e. a product that meets the minimum requirements for a use). The idea is to bring a product to market as early as possible that includes enough features that it can achieve initial benefits, to determine whether the issue is of interest at all (validation of ideas), and to achieve user contact and user feedback as early as possible. In this way, we want to reduce the likelihood of investing in products for which there is no market and gain a better basis for decision-making, which will allow us to deploy our resources in a more targeted manner.

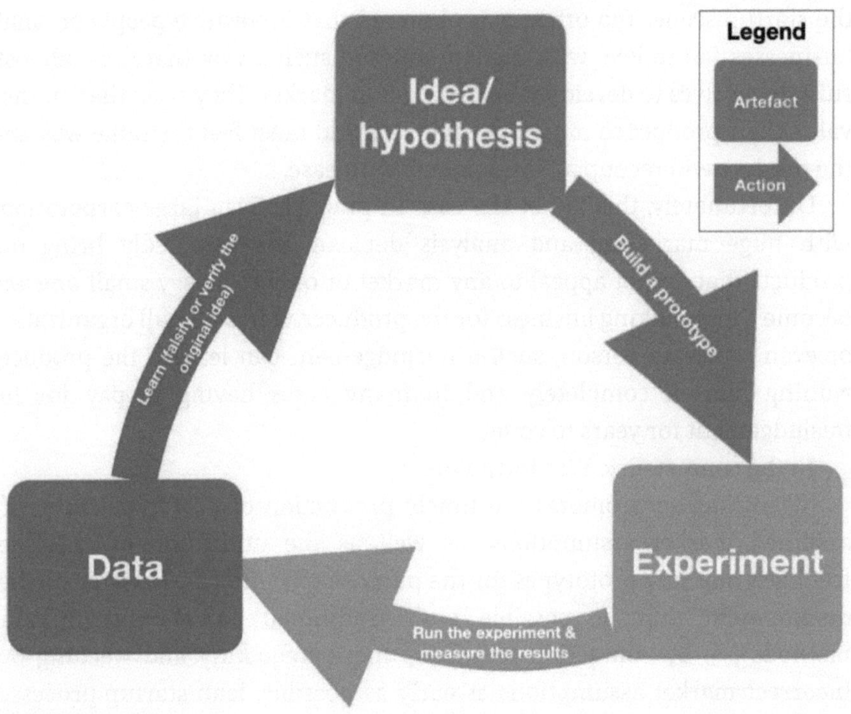

[2]

—

The approach is based on the three stages:

- Learning/planning: We start with a planning phase in which we define what we want to test and compile what information needs exist. An idea or conjecture emerges from the implementation.
- Create: To verify the idea or conjecture, a prototype is built (in the context, an MVP). This creates the basis for an experiment.
- Measure: Conducting experiments and measuring the information obtained in the process generates data, which in turn can be used for further learning. Measurements can be obtained on the one hand based on user data, on the other hand also via specialized software solutions, but also through interviews and surveys.

Experiments on different levels

When creating experiments, we distinguish between prototypes at different levels of implementation. In low fidelity prototypes, we aim to verify a hypothesis simply, quickly, and inexpensively, whereas mid- & high fidelity prototypes demand much higher accuracy and often represent quasi pixel-precise implementations. Coded or live-data based prototypes are another form of enhancement, where real interaction with the system can be approached based on real data and functions. A typical example in practice is A/B testing, in which two functioning solutions are activated in parallel and addressed according to a predefined distribution key. Based on the user behavior in the two variants, for example, one is discarded and the other is developed further.

Feedback and research

The next phase is to put the MVP created and any individual experiments created to the test. Much of what has happened so far has been largely based on assumptions and activities based on them. Now a validation process is on the horizon, in which we use a wide variety of techniques and procedures to verify the hypotheses made based on the MVPs developed from them and seek feedback for them.

In the combination of Lean UX and Scrum we have a very special opportunity here. We do not carry out the process BEFORE the implementation, but WHILE we realize the corresponding requirements. It is therefore a parallel sub-process within the Scrum Sprint, which has the great advantage that we can fully access the findings from the implementation and thus comply with the 2nd principle of the agile manifesto in a particularly goal-oriented manner:

"Welcome requirements changes even late in development. Agile processes leverage change to the customer's competitive advantage."

Needless to say, this review should also be conducted as a collaborative research and evaluation process rather than by individual heroes or experts.

So we take a Continuous Learning approach, where we synergistically gain insights based on the simplest possible approaches and methods as a team.

[1] Translated, "A design system is the central registry that brings together all the elements that enable teams to design, realize and develop a product."

[2] Source: Antonsk, CC BY-SA 4.0 <https://creativecommons.org/licenses/by-sa/4.0>, via Wikimedia Commons

THREE

Dual-Track Agile

Dual-track Agile is a product development methodology in which a cross-functional team divides its daily activities into two parallel tracks - Discovery and Delivery. Unlike standard Agile methodologies where all project members follow the same flow, in Dual-Track Agile, project team members follow a non-linear flow with independent sprints that can vary in length - team members are split between Discovery or Delivery and given a specific project role that comes with its own specific tasks.

In dual-track Agile, team members, which can include designers and developers, work in parallel on discovery and delivery, which allows the team to implement new features into the product while testing new ideas and creating a roadmap for future upgrades.

Even though it appears that the two tracks are divided, the project members working on each of the tracks constantly provide each other with information about their progress so that everyone has a general overview of the current status of the project. It is and remains a joint team, which also shares responsibility for delivering customer value, and realizes this at different times based on different tasks.

Discovery and Delivery Track are based on different backlogs and realize value creation in different ways for the emerging product.

Discovery Track

In traditional projects, product discovery consists of a series of activities carried out during the initial phase of the project - it is usually a single phase that lasts a few weeks or months (depending on the size of the project) before the solution ideas generated in it are implemented as part of development.

When it comes to product development in an increasingly agile, global and ever-changing environment, this approach is not enough, because market opportunities and user expectations often change very quickly ... and no one wants to invest months of development time in an untested functionality that no one wants or even needs.

Dual-track Agile takes a completely different approach. Instead of discovery as a single phase at the beginning or even before the project starts, it becomes a continuous phase that precedes delivery and serves as a guide for the entire project.

Discovery track activities primarily revolve around conducting research, gathering information, and extracting and evaluating insights - all with the goal of creating a production roadmap for the product to best support the realization of the product vision.

Delivery Track

In dual-track Agile, implementation revolves around leveraging all the insights gathered in the Discovery Track to deliver a working product or functionality to users as quickly as possible and further increase value and appeal.

In this track, designers and developers work with users to shape and refine the final product.

Benefit

Dual-track Agile enables long-term product development by maximizing the value that designers, developers, and business strategists bring to the product. Rather than just using it to program, design, or create strategies, by implementing it into the project, it allows the entire team to participate in both the discovery aspect and the delivery aspect of product development. However, in doing so, the work is organized in such a way that this does not reduce the focus of the team and team members on the final product, but on the other hand, it creates a much broader identification with the product that is not only implemented by the team, but also co-designed by the team.

The key to making dual-track Agile work is to set it up as one process and one team working across two tracks, rather than running two processes, two teams, and two tracks that are disconnected.

When implemented properly and in a meaningful project, dual-track Agile accelerates development and release cycles and demonstrates a much faster response to emerging changes in the market or other conditions.

FOUR

COMBINE LEAN UX AND SCRUM

Jeff Gothelf, co-author of the standard work on Lean UX, describes in an article the findings he developed in collaboration with his co-author Josh Seiden and experienced members of the Agile and Scrum community[1]. Five interactions are presented, which can be used in collaboration. From the point of view of practice with Scrum, I cannot agree with his explanations in all aspects:

Product Backlog

The product backlog comprises a large number of requirements in varying degrees of concreteness. Some still have a keyword character and, since they do not have a high priority, are located at the lower end of the prioritized artifact; others, which have a higher priority, have already been further elaborated and concretized in the course of refinements. In this context, creative approaches such as design sprints, hypothesis writing, and similar measures from the portfolio of creative methods can be used to find and specify requirements on the one hand and also to determine them more precisely in terms of their customer benefit on the other.

Sprint Planning

In this section, Gothelf writes : "Sprint planning is the day-to-day planning effort for the team. Questions like "What will it look like?", "How will the product flow from screen to screen?", "What exceptions do we need to handle?" can be answered with design tools like Collaborative Sketching (aka "design studios", "charrettes", etc.) and other group brainstorming activities that UX designers are particularly good at supporting."

This seems to be a fundamental error, since sprint planning is not actually daily planning, but planning for the entire sprint. In the implementation, one should also at least check whether questions such as those mentioned are not better addressed before the sprint planning in the context of refinement, since questions can undoubtedly arise from this. I doubt here whether methods such as Charrettes or similar can be carried out within the framework of the limited time of sprint planning due to timeboxing. In my view, corresponding approaches must take place either in the context of refinement before planning, or in the context of implementation during the actual sprint.

It seems much more sensible to me to use the integration sketch included in the article, which introduces techniques such as "collaborative sketching" or "group brainstorming" as part of sprint planning. This makes sense from a technical point of view and can also be implemented realistically within the time available.

Sprint Backlog / Sprint Execution

A variety of tools can be used during sprint execution. We have discussed some topics on this in the Dual-Track Agile chapter. Methods that Gothelf mentions in the framework of the outline already mentioned are: "Wireframe Creation", "Prototyping", "Visual Design", "Qualitative Research", "Copy / Content", "Experiments / MVP".

The Scrum Team

Gothelf describes that only the participation of a full-time designer in the team can ensure that implementation can take place in parallel collaboration with developers, product managers and Scrum masters. This is in fundamental contradiction to the idea that a Scrum team consists of only three roles and that the tasks in the implementation are implemented by a self-organized developer team, which includes all relevant skills. Thus, from a Scrum perspective, one would probably have to demand that people with UX designer skills can be members of Scrum developer teams, but they are just as much a part of this team as those with database , Java or tester skills and do not take on a separate, fourth role.

The Sprint Review

During the sprint review, the results of the sprint are reviewed together with stakeholders. The goal is neither a release/acceptance nor an evaluation, but exclusively learning from what has already been implemented - with the aim of gaining further insights into how the solution can be designed even better in order to achieve an even greater benefit for the customer. In this event, methods such as design reviews, discussions and quantitative analysis can be used.

Not specifically mentioned, but therefore no less important, is undoubtedly the inclusion of the topic of the integration and interaction of Lean UX and Scrum as part of the continuous improvement of the team process in the context of the sprint retrospective.

[1] Original source: https://medium.com/swlh/here-is-how-ux-design-integrates-with-agile-and-scrum-4f3cf8c10e24

FIVE

Lean UX and Agile UX

Especially when we use Lean UX in an agile context, the question sometimes arises as to what Lean UX is, whether there is then also an Agile UX and how the two would be related.

Basically, the question cannot be answered so easily, especially since we have experienced a true inflation of frameworks and methods in the context of innovative and adaptive approaches in recent years. Thus, any attempt to answer the above question will probably always encounter people who agree with it and those who have a different opinion, because they may consider other approaches or evaluate information differently. Nevertheless here now my answer:

When we talk about UX, i.e. user experience design, we are talking about an approach that basically deals with optimizing the interaction of users and systems. This can be done with different approaches, methods and techniques, but always puts the benefit for the user in the foreground of the efforts. The proximity to approaches in the context of Lean and Agile is correspondingly great.

When we talk about Lean UX, procedures and ideas are based to a large extent on the Lean Startup approach as described by Eric Ries in his book of the same name. This approach has developed in the environment of the Startup Movement in the USA. An important point of view that has arisen from this origin is the desire to understand customer interest on the one hand and the needs and desires of the customer on the other hand as the basis for development as early as possible in the development process. A wide variety of approaches and techniques are used to achieve this. These include: MVP (Minimum Viable Product), funnel analyses, interaction with customers, continuous learning. The basis for this is a "Build-Measure-Learn" cycle as the basis for continuous improvement.

In contrast, when we talk about Agile UX, corresponding approaches are generally based on the values and ideas of the Agile Manifesto, whose origins lie in software development, even if the document is used today by techniques and frameworks in different contexts as a basic philosophy. Agile approaches and procedures applied in this context are generally: short cycles (iterations) followed by feedbacks, as well as in the Lean context a definition of value creation based on the needs of the customer, continuous improvement, often combined with approaches such as Scrum or Kanban.

If we now combine Lean UX with Scrum, we could certainly speak of an Agile UX, especially since the two approaches are not really far apart and much agile mindset can be traced back to principles and ideas from the Lean context. In addition, Scrum, for example, is often used in combination with Lean Startup approaches such as an MVP approach in relation to release planning anyway, which is reflected in the use of the user story mapping technique, for example.

SIX

LEAN UX IN THE ORGANIZATION

Lean UX generally traces its origins to Lean Startup, an approach that does not feature a sophisticated leadership concept. So if we want to learn more about leadership in this context, it is probably appropriate to take a step back and look more closely at the leadership ideas of Lean.

Many companies that want to introduce lean management in their organization do not achieve sustainable success. After a short flash in the pan at the beginning, lean programs and initiatives fall asleep again after a short time and lead to a deterioration in quality and continuity due to the discontinuation of previously used procedures and non-compliance with lean approaches.

The reason is simple: Many organizations introduce new concepts without implementing them sustainably. This would require well thought-out change management and continuous exemplification of the values on the part of the leadership. It is not enough for the leadership to give the "order" to now please cultivate a new way of working together. Rather, it is necessary to take people along on this journey, to perceive their questions and fears, and to demonstrate this new type of collaboration to them both by setting a good example and by continually presenting it as important and desirable in the context of communication. In most cases, this requires not only the introduction of new methods, organizational structures and process descriptions, but rather a change in the **lived** corporate culture. Only if employees see on a daily basis that the new way is the desired and goal-oriented way, which is also lived by superiors (who still also fulfill a certain role model function), will they adopt it themselves. If this is **not** the case, employees will quickly come to the conclusion that the corresponding initiative is once again a new fad with which a manager wanted to distinguish himself, but which plays no role in everyday business and can accordingly be neglected.

If we want to introduce Lean approaches in an organization, this results in three levels which should be considered:

- Mindset, vision, strategy and goals
- Implementation: processes and continuous improvements
- Leadership at all levels

Mindset, vision, strategy and goals

In order to benefit maximally from the use of lean approaches, they must be anchored and lived within the strategy. A common mindset and vision are required, which encompasses collaboration within the team as well as with external stakeholders. The nature of the collaboration is reflected on the one hand in the tactical day-to-day work, but also in the joint development and implementation of strategic goals. An important success factor here is an end-to-end approach in which the entire value chain and all parts of the organization are perceived as a value creation process. In contrast, individualized goal cascades, in which goals are created and evaluated on a divisional or departmental basis, often lead to silo formation rather than to optimization of customer benefits and a focus on their realization.

Implementation: processes and continuous improvements

The implementation of lean approaches is about the implementation of value stream oriented process design. Lean UX is part of the entire process and not an isolated solution. Implementation cannot follow a "big bang" approach, but must be implemented step by step as part of continuous improvements. After each step, the benefits and achievement of objectives are evaluated. If successful, the change is maintained. If the goals have not been achieved, a decision must be made as to whether it makes sense to continue along the path taken - because, for example, it simply takes more time to achieve success - or whether a new path should be embarked upon.

Leadership at all levels

In most companies, there is no clearly defined understanding of leadership and no uniform leadership behavior. Many executives have never received any real leadership training as part of their education and training, and there are hardly any companies that offer coaching for people who have just taken on leadership responsibility. Rather, there seems to be a belief that people who have reached a certain level of education automatically have the necessary interpersonal skills and leadership abilities that enable them to successfully fulfill leadership responsibilities. The fact that this is unfortunately not necessarily the case and that "completely different values and behaviors" count, especially at higher management levels, can be seen from a wide variety of examples of business scandals, whereby it can be assumed that the number of those undesirable developments which are perceived by a larger public represents only a vanishingly small percentage of the actual cases (a business lawyer friend who is active in such cases spoke of a low single-digit percentage which would potentially reach a certain public in the context of indictments).

In addition to the situation where people are promoted to managerial positions based on academic degrees, there is also the approach that good professionals who have been successful in their work in implementation are promoted to department managers or similar, assuming that a good carpenter can also lead and be responsible for a group of carpenters. This can be a sensible path if the person in question is supported in building up the necessary skills and experience to do so. In reality, however, there is very often a mere assumption of competence here as well, which is probably mainly due to the fact that leadership and management responsibility are still often well rewarded today, but are not perceived as a skill in their own right that can be learned.

A fundamental influence on the leadership ability and the leadership behavior of employees in companies is the image of the employees represented by the organization and the leader.

Professor Douglas Murray McGregor (September 6, 1906 - October 1, 1964) of the Sloan School of Management at MIT (Massachusetts Institute of Technology) published two theories in 1960, which represent the extent to which the image people have of their employees influences their leadership behavior and thus also the behavior of the people they lead. These are

Theory X and Theory Y.

The theory X and the theory Y

Wikipedia writes the following about the two theories:

"Theory X - the human being is unwilling

Man has an innate aversion to work and tries to avoid it wherever possible. Because of his reluctance to work, he usually needs to be coerced, directed, guided and threatened with punishment in order to make a productive contribution to the achievement of organizational goals. He wants to be "taken by the hand" because he has too little ambition, prefers routine tasks, and seeks security. He shies away from any responsibility. Therefore, the manager must specify every step of action in detail, vigorously instruct and lead, and strictly control. Only in this way is efficient work execution possible. Remuneration alone cannot make people try hard enough. This means that external controls and punishments, as well as coercion, are needed when rules are violated. His behavior is governed by the majority opinion.

The assumptions of Theory X are essentially the same as the assumptions of Taylorism.

Theory Y - the human is engaged

For humans, work has a high value and is an important source of satisfaction, because they are by nature willing to perform and are motivated from within. The most important incentives for work are the satisfaction of ego needs and the pursuit of self-fulfillment. Therefore, conditions must be created that motivate people, for example through more self-determination, greater areas of responsibility, more flexible organizational structures, group and project work, etc. If the person identifies with the goals of the organization, then external controls are not necessary. This is because he will take responsibility and develop his own initiative. Creativity is also encouraged and demanded. Since this individual is committed to the goals of his organization, he will act in favor of the organizational goals. The individual possesses a high degree of imagination, judgment, and ingenuity to solve organizational problems.

The assumptions of Theory Y essentially correspond to assumptions of the human relations concept. Theory Y is consistent with most corporate mission statements."

The publication is particularly explosive because it describes a self-fulfilling prophecy. Where an organization and superiors have a worldview according to Theory X (whether admitted or not), their leadership behavior will be guided by it and leadership will be very tight and directive: In order to lead such unwilling and unmotivated people, there seems to be no alternative to clear and detailed instructions with no room for maneuver of one's own, as well as close-meshed control and associated sanctions for deviations. In such a context, employees will perform "service by the book". Any deviation, personal initiative and further development is dangerous and can lead to sanctions. The originally incorrect assumption thus becomes reality.

In an organization and with supervisors who represent a Theory Y view of human beings, a supervisor will give his team maximum freedom and scope for creativity and will see his task as providing these people with the appropriate framework and, if necessary, the appropriate information. This can also lead to mistakes in individual cases, but it promotes ongoing further development, buy-in and motivation of the employees and thus leads to better results in terms of quality and quantity.

Lean approaches, like agile approaches, require a Theory Y environment. Anyone who tries to implement them in a Theory X environment will inevitably fail, because the foundations for success not only do not exist, but are deliberately made impossible.

Leadership at all levels

A central theme of Lean is leadership at all levels. This is often supplemented by "management levels", but this runs counter to the actual topic. In fact, it is about decisions being made at all levels and responsibility being borne for them. The word "responsibility" does not mean that sanctions should be taken for wrong decisions, but that employees at all levels should perceive themselves as co-creators of the organization, its processes and products. In this context, management should set goals, but leave the implementation decisions to those who actually carry them out. This is about identification and commitment. Where superiors give detailed instructions and largely keep employees away from decisions, employees will always feel "not responsible. After all, they only do what they are told to do and perceive that their knowledge and experience are often only marginally desired or in demand. Commitment is correspondingly low. Only by handing over decision-making responsibility will employees also perceive the work and the products created in the process as "theirs" and (be able to) assume corresponding responsibility. Where this is not the case, a change process must be supported in order to be sustainable.

If we want to successfully implement Lean UX or any other lean- or agile-based approach, commitment and ownership is always a key success factor and supervisors and organizations need to adapt their leadership and collaboration accordingly.

I often see that supervisors are afraid to hand over responsibility because they fear failure and the resulting disadvantages for the organization as well as for themselves and their work.

SEVEN

The Scrum.org PSU Certification

The Professional Scrum™ with User Experience (PSU I) certification can be achieved by successfully passing the corresponding certification exam through Scrum.org. The exam is presented as a Level I exam, with no further levels based on it announced or offered at the time of publication of the book.

Based on the still extremely low number of PSU-I certified persons (less than 2000 worldwide after more than two and a half years), this is not expected to change in the foreseeable future. At the same time, the small number of corresponding certifications is definitely an advantage for persons who have successfully passed the examination. They are therefore not competing with hundreds of thousands of people like, for example, people who have a PSM-I, i.e. a Scrum Master certification from Scrum.org (as of the end of 2021, just under 435,000 people), but are part of an exclusive circle of specialists.

Anyone who wants to obtain PSU certification can do so by ordering an exam voucher on the Scrum.org website. This letter-number code is sent by email after payment (by credit card or Paypal) within a maximum of one working day. It is valid for an unlimited period of time and cost US$ 200 at the time of writing. There are no other requirements to take the exam. Thus, there is NO obligation to participate in a specific training course or the like. Those who answer more than 85% of the questions correctly within the available time will be certified. It does not matter whether the preparation was done in self-study or in a training course. Before booking the exam, it is necessary to register on the website, if not already registered.

The corresponding menu item is offered on the main page of the website www.scrum.org.

The exam consists of 60 questions, which must be answered within 60 minutes, which means a reduction of 20 questions compared to PSM-I or PSPO-I (where 80 questions are asked in 60 minutes). The exam takes place completely online and can be taken at any time after entering a code. There is no reservation of a certain exam period and the exam takes place without video surveillance or similar. All desired materials may be used (open book), but this is put into perspective by the demanding pace of an average of one question per minute.

True/false, multiple choice and multiple answer questions are used (no open questions, only questions for ticking). In the exam there is a possibility to set flags, and as long as the exam lasts, once answered questions can also be improved. Correctly answered questions are awarded one point at the end of the exam (regardless of whether one or more answers had to be marked), incorrectly answered or unanswered questions count as "0". It is therefore recommended to answer all questions and, if necessary, to guess if an answer was not known. The exam is currently only offered in English, other languages can be selected by using a Google Translate plugin. Of course Scrum.org cannot be held responsible for the quality of the translation of a third party provider.

The information whether the test has been passed is displayed immediately after the test. In this case, the corresponding certificate can be downloaded together with the badge in the registered customer area of the website after a few days. The certificate only shows that the exam has been passed. The score is displayed separately. An evaluation according to individual questions is not handed over. If the exam was not passed, it can be taken a second time after remitting the exam costs. Scrum.org does not know any limitation of the number of attempts, which may be spent, but requires a new examination fee for each further attempt. Some course providers offer in the context of their offers that an exam can be repeated free of charge within a certain period of time in case of failure. However, one may at least assume that in this case the corresponding "risk" on the part of the school is taken into account within the framework of its pricing.

To prepare for the exam, a number of providers offer sample questions for a fee. I have noticed with some checks that these are very good and purposeful with some providers, but in some other cases unfortunately have little to do with the subject. It is therefore advisable to look around for appropriate references before purchasing.

Printed by Libri Plureos GmbH in Hamburg,
Germany